Know the Rules UK

A Straightforward Guide to Work, Renting, Driving, and Everyday Life

Bukky Okunade

Published by Find A Fresh Publishing

ISBN 978-1-0684655-0-5

Important Disclaimer

The purpose of this book is to give readers a general understanding of everyday systems, services, and responsibilities in the UK. We have done our best to ensure the information is accurate, but laws and regulations may change.

The content should not be taken as legal advice or a substitute for professional guidance. The author and publisher accept no liability for actions taken based on the material in this book. Readers are encouraged to consult qualified professionals, official sources, or legal advisers for guidance specific to their situation.

Dedication

This book is dedicated to everyone who just wanted to get things right but didn't know where to start.

Contents

INTRODUCTION

Welcome to *Know the Rules UK: A Straightforward Guide to Work, Renting, Driving, and Everyday Life*. Whether you have recently come to the UK or have been here for a long time and want to understand how things work, this book is here to help you live with more confidence, clarity, and control.

Life in a new country, or even in your own country when entering adulthood, can feel overwhelming at times. Rules, responsibilities, and systems can seem complicated, especially if they are not explained clearly. Know the Rules UK provides step-by-step explanations for various areas such as renting a flat, registering with a GP, handling everyday paperwork, and avoiding common legal mistakes.

Think of this book as your everyday guidebook for getting on with life in the UK. It's not a textbook or a legal manual; it's a practical handbook that is clear, simple, and direct.

Who This Book Is For

This book is designed for anyone who needs a clearer understanding of how to live and thrive in the UK. That includes

- **Newcomers to the UK**: Whether you've moved here from abroad to work, study, or join family, this book gives you a head start on understanding how daily life operates, from registering with a GP to understanding council tax.
- **Young adults leaving home**: If you're moving out for the first time, starting a job, or managing your bills, this guide helps you step into independence with more confidence.
- **Students**: Whether you're a home or an international student, knowing how to rent safely, work part-time, and access health services is vital.
- **People in transition**: If you're going through changes like starting a new job, applying for benefits, or learning to drive, this book will walk you through what you need to know and do.
- **Anyone who's ever thought, "Why didn't someone explain this earlier?"** This book is for you.

What You'll Learn

Each chapter focuses on a key part of daily life, with tips to help you deal with things more appropriately. You'll learn about:

- Renting safely and knowing your rights as a tenant
- Working legally and understanding your payslip and employment terms

- Registering with a GP and knowing what healthcare is free
- Opening a bank account, using credit wisely, and avoiding debt traps
- Staying safe online and offline
- Understanding your legal rights, personal responsibilities, and where to get help

This book gives you the essentials to live well, avoid costly mistakes, and feel more in control of your everyday life.

How to Use This Book

You don't need to read every page consecutively. Each chapter stands alone and is designed so you can dip in and out depending on what you need at any given time. Whether you're looking for your first flat, starting a new job, or trying to understand council tax, there's a chapter for that.

Use this book as a practical reference guide. You can highlight key sections, make your own notes, or return to certain pages as your situation changes. It helps you through all stages of life in the UK, from arrival to settling in, growing, and taking on new responsibilities.

If it helps, keep a notebook or digital file alongside the book to jot down important numbers, contacts, and next steps as you go.

A Word of Encouragement

You are not expected to know everything from the outset. Living in the UK involves understanding a range of systems, responsibilities, and everyday procedures that can take time to learn. With accessible guidance and reliable information, you can make informed choices and approach new situations with greater confidence.

If you have ever found official information unclear or felt unsure about where to begin, this book is here to offer clarity. It is designed to be practical, respectful of your experience, and supportive of your independence.

You have the right to understand how things work.

You have the right to make informed decisions.

This book will help you do that.

CHAPTER 1

UNDERSTANDING THE UK SYSTEM

Adjusting to life in the UK can sometimes feel overwhelming. There isn't always a clear starting point, yet there are often essential forms and registrations to complete, services to sign up for, and rules to follow. Information isn't always easy to find, and it's not always obvious which organisation is responsible for what.

Whether you've just arrived or have lived here for years, understanding the structure can make everyday life much easier. When you know how public services are organised, where to go for help, and who does what, you can make decisions with greater confidence and avoid unnecessary delays or confusion.

Some services, like healthcare through the NHS, are managed nationally. Others, such as bin collections, schools, and housing, are run by your local council. Knowing the difference helps you get things sorted without stress.

This chapter provides you with a simple introduction to how public services and government work in the UK. By understanding the key institutions, your rights, and how different systems connect, you'll be better equipped to manage everyday life with confidence.

How the UK is Organised: National, Local, and Devolved Powers

To understand where to go for help, it helps to know how the UK is structured.

At the top is the central government, based in Westminster (London), which is responsible for national matters like taxes, passports, benefits, and immigration. Departments like HMRC (for taxes), DWP (for benefits), and the Home Office (for immigration and security) operate across the whole country.

Below that, there are devolved governments in Scotland, Wales, and Northern Ireland, which control areas such as health, education, and transport in their regions. For instance, the NHS in Scotland operates independently from NHS England, and the education systems also exhibit variations.

Then you have local government, your local council, which handles things like:

- Schools and school admissions
- Rubbish collection and recycling
- Local roads and street lighting
- Council housing and homelessness services
- Social care
- Leisure centres and libraries
- Council Tax

Each local authority operates slightly differently, and different areas may refer to services under different names. You can find your local council's website by entering your postcode at www.gov.uk/find-local-council.

Common Services and Who Handles What

Here's a breakdown of everyday needs and which part of government usually deals with them:

Need or Issue	Who to Contact
Registering with a GP	NHS (through your local GP surgery)
Applying for a school place	Your local council
Universal Credit, Jobseeker's Allowance	Department for Work and Pensions (DWP)
Income tax or National Insurance questions	HM Revenue & Customs (HMRC)
Reporting antisocial behaviour in your area	Local council or local police (101)
Road tax or updating your driving licence	DVLA (Driver and Vehicle Licensing Agency)
Passport applications	HM Passport Office
Help with housing or homelessness	Local council Housing Department

If you're not sure who to contact, start at www.gov.uk. It's the official website for UK government services and provides links to the correct departments. Local council websites are also useful for area-specific services.

Getting Your Paperwork in Order

As you settle into life in the UK, you'll almost certainly need a few documents and registrations, regardless of your background:

1. **National Insurance Number (NI number)**
   This is used for working, paying tax, and claiming benefits. If you don't have one, you can apply online at www.gov.uk/apply-national-insurance-number.

2. **Registering with a GP**
   A General Practitioner (GP) is your first point of contact for health services. You do this by contacting a GP surgery near your home. If possible, bring proof of your ID and address; however, GPs can still register you even if you do not have these documents.

3. **Bank Account**
   Most employers and landlords will expect you to have a UK bank account. You'll usually need ID and proof of address to open one. Some banks also allow you to use official letters from Jobcentre Plus or your college if you're a student.

4. **Council Tax Account**
   If you're renting or buying a home, you'll need to set up a Council Tax account with your local council. This pays for services like rubbish collection and street

lighting. Discounts or exemptions are available if you live alone, are a student, or have a low income.

5. **Right to Work and Immigration Documents**
   If you're not a UK citizen, make sure your visa or immigration status is up to date. Most employers now check your right to work using the Home Office's digital system.

Keep copies of all official letters, receipts, and reference numbers. You'll find them useful more often than you anticipate.

Avoiding Common Mistakes

Many people delay getting organised because they assume someone will explain everything in time, but that often doesn't happen. Some of the most common issues include:

- Missing deadlines for school admissions or housing applications
- Getting charged the wrong Council Tax because your household details weren't updated
- Facing delays in benefit payments because forms were incomplete or missing documentation
- Missing healthcare appointments due to not being registered with a GP

These aren't mistakes caused by laziness. They happen because the system is complex, and it's easy to assume you're not doing anything urgent. But getting things sorted early saves time, stress, and money.

Helpful Tools and Where to Go for Support

The good news is, there are free, trusted places where you can get guidance:

www.gov.uk	This is the official website of the UK government. Use this to access services, find contact details, and apply for documents.
Your local council website	Use www.gov.uk/find-local-council to find yours.
Citizens Advice	They provide free assistance both online and in person regarding housing, employment, benefits, and other topics. Visit www.citizensadvice.org.uk.
Jobcentre Plus	If you're unemployed or on a low income, this is where to go for support with benefits and job-seeking.
NHS.uk	For GP and dentist registration, health advice, and contact information for local services, visit this page.

CHAPTER 2

WORKING IN THE UK

Earning a living in the UK can take many forms, whether through employment, self-employment, or starting your own business. Whatever path you choose, it's vital to understand your rights, how income is taxed, and how to spot and handle common challenges in the workplace or while working for yourself.

This chapter will help you prepare for job hunting or self-employment, stay safe at work, and seek help. You'll also get tips on finding opportunities, understanding the job market, and building a stable, rewarding working life in the UK.

Types of Employment

Understanding your employment status is crucial because it directly affects your pay, taxes, benefits, and legal protections. The main employment categories include being employed, self-employed, working through an agency, or on a zero-hours contracts.

- **Employed**
  You work for an employer who pays you a salary or an hourly wage. Your employer deducts tax and National Insurance contributions from your pay through the PAYE (Pay As You Earn) system.
- **Self-Employed**
  You run your own business or work freelance. You are responsible for reporting your income and paying tax

and National Insurance directly to HMRC using the Self-Assessment system.

- **Agency or Zero-Hours Work**
  You work through a recruitment agency or on a flexible, ad hoc basis without guaranteed hours. Even so, you have rights such as holiday pay and the national minimum wage, depending on your contract.

Avoiding Job Scams and Exploitation

Before you start applying for jobs, it's essential to know that not all offers are genuine or fair. Most UK employers follow the law, but some exploit job seekers, especially those who are new to the country, young, or unfamiliar with the system.

Spotting Job Scams

Job scams often appear legitimate at first. Scammers use convincing tactics to get personal details or money from people looking for work. They might create fake job adverts, pretend to be recruitment agents, or contact you through messaging apps like WhatsApp or social media.

Common warning signs include:

- Offers of high pay with little or no experience required
- Requests for upfront payments for training, equipment, or "processing fees"

- Jobs offered without an interview or a proper application process
- Pressure to accept quickly or keep the offer secret
- Poor spelling or grammar in adverts or emails
- Requests for sensitive personal details early on, such as bank information or a passport scan

In recent cases, victims have lost hundreds or even thousands of pounds to these scams. For instance, scammers have used fake warehouse job offers to trick people into paying fees or agreeing to exploitative work conditions.

How to Stay Safe When Job Hunting

You can take some simple steps to protect yourself:

- Only use trusted websites and official job platforms such as Jobcentre Plus
- Research companies using their official website or the Companies House register
- Never pay money upfront for a job or training unless it's through a trusted provider
- Don't give personal or financial information too early in the process
- Be cautious if a job offer seems too good to be true

If you come across a suspicious job ad, report it to **Action Fraud** (www.actionfraud.police.uk) or get help from Citizens Advice.

Recognising Exploitation

Sometimes, what starts as a real job turns out to be exploitative. This can include:

- Being paid below the legal minimum wage
- Being charged for uniforms, travel, or accommodation without your agreement
- Working without a written contract or payslip ("cash in hand")
- Being placed in overcrowded or poor living conditions tied to your job

The Gangmasters and Labour Abuse Authority (GLAA) uncovered cases in 2023 where employers charged recruitment fees and gave workers illegal or exploitative jobs. This shows how important it is to be cautious, even when the job seems real.

Finding Work

Finding a job in the UK can be straightforward if you know where to look and how to apply. Online job boards such as Indeed, Reed, and the government's own Jobcentre Plus website offer thousands of vacancies. Recruitment agencies can also help match your skills with employers.

A well-prepared CV and cover letter can make a difference. Your CV should highlight your skills, experience, and qualifications clearly and honestly. When invited to interviews, research the company and be ready to discuss your strengths and how you fit the role.

Where to Look

- **Job websites**: Indeed, Reed, CV-Library, Totaljobs
- **Government portal**: Find a job service
- **Agencies**: Reputable employment agencies can help with temporary or permanent work
- **LinkedIn**: A professional profile can open doors, especially for skilled roles

What You'll Need

- National Insurance (NI) number
- CV (curriculum vitae) summarising your experience
- Proof of right-to-work (passport, visa, or biometric residence permit)
- UK bank account to receive your pay

Understanding Your Rights at Work

The UK has strong legal protections for workers, including:

- The right to a written contract and payslips showing pay and deductions
- Payment of at least the National Minimum Wage
- Holiday pay (at least 28 days for full-time workers)
- Rest breaks and limits on working hours

- Protection against unfair dismissal (after two years of continuous employment)
- Statutory sick pay if you earn above the threshold (currently £123+ per week)
- Time off for illness or emergencies
- Maternity and paternity leave for eligible employees

Part-time, agency, and zero-hours workers have many of the same rights, but some differences apply depending on the contract.

Organisations like ACAS (Advisory, Conciliation and Arbitration Service) offer free advice and dispute resolution support if you believe you have received unfair treatment.

For more information, visit gov.uk/your-employment-rights.

Payslips, Tax, and National Insurance (NI)

When you work in the UK, you are required to pay income tax and National Insurance (NI) contributions. If you are employed, your employer will handle these payments on your behalf by deducting the correct amounts from your wages through the Pay As You Earn (PAYE) system. Your payslip will show details such as your gross pay, the amount of income tax and NI deducted, and any pension contributions if you are enrolled in a workplace pension scheme.

If you are self-employed, you are responsible for reporting your income and paying the correct amount of tax and NI yourself. This is done through an annual self-assessment tax return submitted to HM Revenue and Customs (HMRC). You must register with HMRC, keep clear and accurate records of all income and allowable business expenses, and meet key deadlines, usually by 31 January each year, to avoid penalties or interest charges. Good recordkeeping is essential to ensure your tax return is accurate and complete.

Managing Self-Employment

As a self-employed person, being organised is key to keeping your business running smoothly. Beyond completing your work, you'll need to stay on top of your income and expenses. Simple tools like spreadsheets or bookkeeping apps can help you track your income and expenses, making it easier to calculate how much tax and National Insurance you owe.

Planning ahead for deadlines is important. The most significant date is 31 January, when your online self-assessment and tax payment for the previous year are both due. Setting reminders and keeping your records up to date throughout the year can help prevent last-minute stress.

If you're unsure about the process, you don't have to do it alone. Many people find it helpful to speak to an accountant, especially when their business starts growing or becomes more complex. The goal is to stay in control and avoid unexpected costs or penalties while focusing on the work you enjoy.

Why Having an Accountant Can Help if You Are Self-Employed

If managing your finances feels overwhelming, working with an accountant can make a big difference. They bring expert knowledge of tax rules, allowable expenses, and reporting requirements, helping you stay compliant while making the most of what you earn.

Beyond filing your self-assessment, an accountant can help you plan, advising on things like pension contributions, which not only prepare you for the future but may also reduce your tax bill. They can also support you with budgeting, setting up a reliable bookkeeping system, and managing cash flow, giving you more clarity and control over your business finances.

Finding a qualified accountant is easier than you might think. Professional bodies like the Association of Chartered Certified Accountants (ACCA) and the Institute of Chartered Accountants in England and Wales (ICAEW) maintain directories of certified accountants. While it may feel like an extra cost at first, a good accountant can save you time, reduce stress, and help ensure you're not paying more tax than necessary, making it a wise investment in your business.

Planning for the Future: National Insurance and Pensions

While your focus may be on your earnings today, it's important to understand how some of the deductions from your income, especially National Insurance (NI) and pension contributions, are actually helping to build your financial security for the future.

Understanding National Insurance

National Insurance is a system of contributions paid by workers and the self-employed. These payments go towards funding state benefits such as the State Pension, maternity allowance, and certain unemployment or sickness benefits. You start paying NI once your income passes certain thresholds. If you're employed, this starts when you earn over £1,048 a month; if self-employed, it begins when your profits exceed £12,570 a year.

Your NI payments build up what's known as "qualifying years." These determine whether you're eligible for certain benefits, particularly the State Pension. To receive the full State Pension, you generally need around 35 qualifying years. If you have less than that, your pension will be cut, and you usually need at least 10 years to receive a benefit.

You can earn qualifying years by working and paying NI, receiving eligible benefits, or making voluntary NI contributions to fill any gaps. It's a good habit to check your NI record regularly to ensure you're on track. You can do this easily at gov.uk/check-national-insurance.

State Pension and Why It Matters

The state pension is a regular payment from the government once you reach the state pension age (currently 66), but it may change in the future. It's not automatic; it depends entirely on how many qualifying years you've built up through your NI contributions. It's imperative to monitor your NI history if you have not worked continuously, have been self-employed, or have taken time off for caregiving. You can get a forecast of what you're likely to receive, and when, by visiting gov.uk/check-state-pension.

Workplace Pensions: A Boost from Your Employer

In addition to the state pension, most employees enrol in a workplace pension scheme. If you're aged 22 or over and earn at least £10,000 a year, your employer is legally required to enrol you automatically. This means that every payday, a percentage of your wages is contributed to a pension pot. Your employer also contributes, usually at least 3%, and the government adds tax relief, giving your savings a helpful boost.

You do have the option to opt out, but unless you have another strong retirement plan, staying enrolled is typically the smarter choice. You're effectively receiving free money from your employer and the government towards your future. To explore your options or estimate how much you could save over time, visit moneyhelper.org.uk.

Why This Is Worth Paying Attention To

Pensions may seem like a distant concern, but the earlier you understand and engage with how they work, the better prepared you'll be. Many people don't realise until late in life that they haven't earned enough NI years or have missed out on employer contributions. If your work history includes part-time jobs, career breaks, or periods of self-employment, checking your records regularly can help you take action early, whether by topping up missing contributions or making informed decisions about your future plans.

CHAPTER 3

MONEY, BANKING, AND YOUR RIGHTS

Money plays a central role in daily life, from where you live and how you get around to managing bills, debt, and your future. But in the UK, it's not just about how much money you have. Understanding how the financial system works, your rights as a consumer, and how to stay protected can make a big difference to your well-being and peace of mind.

This chapter guides you through the essentials: opening a bank account, using credit responsibly, recognising scams, dealing with debt, and knowing where to turn for help if things go wrong.

Understanding the UK Banking System

Most financial transactions in the UK rely on having a personal bank account. Wages, benefits, and pensions are paid into bank accounts by default. It's also the safest way to pay bills and manage money.

The UK banking system is made up of high street banks (like Barclays, HSBC, NatWest, and Lloyds), online-only banks (such as Monzo or Starling), and credit unions (community-based financial services that can offer ethical banking and loans).

Banking Features:

Current Accounts	Everyday accounts used for spending, receiving money, paying bills, and direct debits.

Savings Accounts	For putting money aside and earning interest.
Debit Cards	Linked to current accounts for cash withdrawal and spending.
Bank Transfers	Fast and commonly used through online or mobile banking apps.

You can manage most banking through online apps, but branches still exist for in-person help.

Opening a Bank Account

To open a UK bank account, you usually need:

- Proof of identity (e.g., passport, biometric residence card, or UK driving licence)
- Proof of address (e.g., utility bill, council tax letter, tenancy agreement)

If you're new to the UK or don't have all the usual documents, you can:

- Look into **basic bank accounts** with fewer requirements
- Try online banks like Monese or Revolut
- Join a **credit union**, which may offer more flexibility

Some high street banks also offer special accounts for newcomers or people rebuilding credit.

Budgeting and Managing Everyday Expenses

The cost of living in the UK varies widely by region, but careful budgeting helps you avoid debt and plan for the unexpected.

Start by tracking:

- Essential costs: rent, food, travel, utilities
- Non-essentials: subscriptions, takeaways, social spending
- Occasional costs: school items, gifts, annual renewals

Free budgeting apps like Emma, Plum or Snoop can help you manage spending. Some local councils and charities also run workshops or offer advice on budgeting and saving.

Understanding Credit and Loans

Credit means borrowing money now and paying it back later, often with interest. You might use credit for:

- Phone contracts
- Credit cards or overdrafts
- Car finance or personal loans
- Mortgages or "Buy Now, Pay Later" services

Your credit score (held by agencies like Experian, Equifax, and TransUnion) affects whether you can borrow and on what terms. You can check your score for free online.

Used carefully, credit can be useful, but missed payments can damage your record and lead to fees or legal action. Always read the terms and compare lenders before borrowing.

Dealing with Debt and Getting Help

If you're struggling with repayments, don't ignore the problem. Financial difficulties can affect anyone, and acting early can make a big difference. Warning signs that debt may be becoming unmanageable include relying on credit to cover everyday essentials, missing rent or council tax payments, or avoiding contact with lenders and creditors.

Free and confidential help is available from trusted organisations. StepChange, Citizens Advice, and National Debtline all offer advice, tools, and personalised support to help you understand your options and take control. If you're eligible, schemes like Breathing Space can offer temporary protection from creditor action, giving you 60 days to get advice and put a plan in place without added pressure.

Recognising and Avoiding Financial Scams

Scams are a growing problem in the UK, with UK Finance reporting that individuals lost over £1.2 billion due to scams and fraud in 2022. These scams are becoming increasingly sophisticated and often target people online or by phone. Criminals may impersonate banks, government departments, or delivery companies to steal personal information or money.

Common scams include:

- Fake text messages from "Royal Mail" or "HMRC"
- Cryptocurrency or investment scams promising high returns
- Romance scams on dating sites
- Loan or job scams asking for upfront payments

Protect yourself by:

- Never sharing personal details or PINs by phone or email
- Avoiding links from unknown senders
- Only shopping on secure websites (look for the padlock and https://)
- Reporting suspicious messages to www.gov.uk/report-suspicious-emails-websites-phishing

If money is taken from your account without permission, report it to your bank immediately and contact Action Fraud at www.actionfraud.police.uk.

Understanding Your Consumer Rights

Strong laws protect consumers in the UK when they purchase goods or services, whether in stores or online.

You have the right to:

- A refund or replacement for faulty goods within 30 days
- Cancel online purchases within 14 days (a legal "cooling-off" period)
- Clear information about prices and no hidden charges
- Products or services that match their description

Keep receipts or order confirmations and take screenshots of adverts or listings where needed.

If you feel you've been treated unfairly:

- Contact Citizens Advice. Consumer Service
- Report serious issues to your local Trading Standards office

Extra Protection When Shopping with Cards

If you pay by card, especially a credit card, you may have extra rights if something goes wrong.

- Section 75 of the Consumer Credit Act protects purchases between £100 and £30,000 made using a credit card. If the retailer doesn't deliver, the card company may refund you.
- Chargeback allows debit and credit card payments to be reversed if you didn't receive the goods or were overcharged.

What to Do If Something Goes Wrong

Take immediate action to address any overcharging, misrepresentation, or unfair treatment.

1. Contact the company directly to explain the problem and ask for a resolution. This method can resolve many issues.
2. If the issue isn't resolved, seek free, unbiased advice on your rights and next steps by contacting Citizens Advice.
3. You may be able to contact the relevant Ombudsman Service to help settle the matter without going to court.
4. If you have encountered fraud or a scam, promptly report it to your bank and Action Fraud at www.actionfraud.police.uk.

Understanding your rights and following the proper process gives you a strong chance of getting a fair outcome.

CHAPTER 4

FINDING A PLACE TO LIVE

Finding somewhere to live is a big step and often one of the most stressful parts of adult life, especially if you're unfamiliar with the UK rental system. From paperwork and legal terms to deposits and landlord responsibilities, there's a lot to take in.

This chapter explains the essentials, what to expect when renting, the documents you'll need, and how to avoid common problems like scams or unfair treatment. Whether you're a student, relocating for work, moving in with others, or searching for a long-term home, understanding your rights and responsibilities as a tenant can make the process much smoother and more secure.

Types of Housing in the UK

Most people looking for somewhere to live will be choosing between two main options:

- Renting from a private landlord or through a letting agent
- Applying for council or housing association housing (also known as social housing)

Private Renting

This includes renting an entire flat or house or sharing with others in a house-share or HMO (House in Multiple Occupation). Many properties are managed by letting agents on behalf of landlords. Letting agents must follow legal standards and fair practices, such as protecting your deposit and providing accurate information.

Social Housing

Social housing is usually more affordable than private renting, but it is limited and based on need. You must apply through your local council, and you may be placed on a waiting list. Priority is typically given to those with urgent housing needs, such as low income, disability, overcrowding, or homelessness.

You can learn more or apply at gov.uk/apply-for-council-housing

What to Expect When Renting

Here are the usual steps to renting a place privately in the UK:

1. **Search for property**
   Use websites like Rightmove, Zoopla, or SpareRoom for house shares.

2. **View the property**
   Visit in person if possible. Check for dampness, working appliances, locks, and fire safety. Ask what's included in the rent (e.g., bills, internet).

3. **Provide documents**
   You'll usually need:
   - Photo ID (passport or driving licence)
   - Proof of income or employment
   - References from previous landlords
   - Visa or immigration status, if applicable

4. **Pay a holding deposit**
   This is usually capped at one week's rent. It shows you're serious, and the landlord agrees to take the property off the market while checks are done.

5. **Pass reference checks**
   The landlord or agent may check your credit history and right to rent in the UK.

6. **Pay a security deposit and sign a tenancy agreement**
   The **security deposit** is usually no more than five weeks' rent. It must be protected in a government-approved scheme (more on that below).

Your Rights as a Tenant

When renting a home in the UK, the law gives you important rights:

- You have the right to **live in a safe, well-maintained property**.
- Your **landlord must give you at least 24 hours' notice** before visiting.
- Your **security deposit must be protected** in a registered scheme (TDS, DPS, or MyDeposits). You should get proof within 30 days.
- You must receive a copy of:
  - **Your tenancy agreement**
  - The **'How to Rent' guide** (available on gov.uk)
  - The property's **gas safety certificate**
  - The **Energy Performance Certificate (EPC)**

Common Pitfalls to Avoid

A Surge in Scams

Rental fraud is increasing in the UK. In 2023, Action Fraud recorded over 5,000 cases, with average losses of around £1,400 per victim, and some people lost as much as £20,000.

Common Scam Tactics

- Fake listings advertising suspiciously low rent
- Pressure tactics urging you to pay before seeing the property
- Borrowed photos from legitimate sites reused in fake ads

- Virtual viewings only, with excuses for not allowing in-person visits
- Untraceable payment methods such as Western Union, MoneyGram, or cash

Real-Life Fraud Cases

- A London student paid a £1,000 deposit via Facebook Marketplace, only to arrive and find a stranger living at the address
- A couple lost £8,100 after scammers used a fake letting agent and Airbnb-style photos to trick them

Tips to Stay Safe

- Always view the property in person before paying any money
- Verify the identity of the landlord or letting agent through official contact details
- Use secure payment methods like bank transfers, avoiding cash or money transfer services
- Be cautious of deals that seem too good to be true, especially unusually low rent
- Check the property's listing on multiple websites to spot duplicates or inconsistencies
- Ask for a written tenancy agreement and read it carefully before signing
- Report suspicious listings or contacts to Action Fraud or your local council

What About Council Housing?

If you are on a low income or facing urgent housing needs, you can apply for council housing. Each council has its own criteria, but generally, you need to:

- Be on a low income or receiving benefits
- Have lived in the area for a certain period
- Have a valid reason for needing social housing, such as overcrowding or an unsafe current home

Social housing can take time to access, but some housing associations also offer shared ownership schemes. These shared ownership schemes help people purchase a portion of a home when they cannot afford to pay the full price.

Where to Get Help

If you're struggling to find a place to live or believe your landlord is acting unfairly, support is available from:

- **Shelter**: Expert advice on housing and homelessness www.shelter.org.uk | 0808 800 4444
- **Citizens Advice**: Free help with housing, deposits, and legal rights www.citizensadvice.org.uk
- **Your local council**: Assistance with homelessness prevention, housing applications, and landlord enforcement

Chapter 5

Healthcare, GP Registration, and the NHS

Good health is the foundation of a stable and fulfilling life. Understanding how the healthcare system works is essential to living in the UK. The National Health Service (NHS) provides a wide range of services, most of which are free at the point of use. But to access care smoothly, you need to know how to register, what to expect from different services, and when to use them. This chapter will help you feel ready to take care of your health.

What Is the NHS, and How Does It Work?

The NHS is a publicly funded healthcare system paid for through taxes and National Insurance. It includes hospitals, GP surgeries, pharmacies, and community services. Most treatment is free at the point of use, but there are a few things you might need to pay for.

There are slight differences across the UK:

- England: Prescriptions cost a standard fee (around £9.35 per item). There are also charges for dental and eye care.
- Scotland, Wales, and Northern Ireland: Prescriptions are free. Dental and eye care may also be free or reduced, depending on income and age.

Emergency NHS care is free for anyone in the UK at the time of needing it, no matter your immigration status.

Registering with a GP

Registering with a GP (General Practitioner) is the first step to using the NHS for everyday healthcare. Your GP is the main person you will see for check-ups, prescriptions, ongoing medical conditions, and referrals to specialists.

1. Find a local GP surgery using your postcode at www.nhs.uk.
2. You need essential documents like a passport or photo ID and evidence of your address, like a utility bill or tenancy agreement.
3. Fill in a registration form. You may be asked for proof of immigration or refugee status.
4. Get your NHS number: Once registered, you will be assigned an NHS number. This will appear on appointment letters and prescriptions and is yours for life.
5. Book your first appointment: Let the practice know about ongoing medical conditions or medications to ensure continuity of care.

If you move home, you should register with a new GP in your local area. You can keep the same GP until treatment is complete, but it is usually easier to change.

Health Support for Migrants, Refugees, and Visitors

Whether you're visiting, temporarily staying, or settling long-term in the UK, here's what you need to know about NHS access and costs depending on your immigration or residency status.

Immigration Health Surcharge (IHS)

If you're coming to the UK for more than six months on a visa (such as work, study, family, or youth mobility), you're usually required to pay the Immigration Health Surcharge (IHS) as part of your visa application. This gives you full access to NHS services on the same basis as residents for the duration of your visa.

- **2025 rates**: £1,035 per year for most adult applicants; £776 per year for students and youth mobility visas
- **Who's exempt**: Health and care workers (with relevant visa), asylum seekers, refugees, those applying for indefinite leave to remain, victims of trafficking or domestic violence, and some other specific groups
- **Surcharge refunds**: You can get a refund if your visa is refused or withdrawn, but not in other cases, such as death prior to entry

What You Can Access (Based on Your Status)

Your Status	Do You Pay IHS?	GP & Emergency (A&E)	Hospital and Specialist Care
Visitor (less than 6 months)	No	Free	You must pay (usually 150% of the NHS cost)
Visa holder (6+ months with IHS)	Yes	Free	Free (standard charges like prescriptions still apply)
Asylum seeker or refugee	No	Free	Free
Settled or 'ordinarily resident'	No	Free	Free

Important: A&E (accident and emergency) care and GP consultations are free for everyone, even if you are here temporarily or your visa has expired.

Medical Interpreters

If English is not your first language, you can ask for a medical interpreter when visiting the GP or hospital. Some NHS services offer this for free. Local charities and migrant support groups may also provide interpreters.

When to Use GPs, Walk-In Centres, NHS 111, and A&E

Knowing where to go for healthcare makes a big difference. It saves you time, reduces stress, and ensures that emergency services are available for serious cases.

GP Surgery	For ongoing health concerns, prescriptions, check-ups, and referrals.
Walk-In Centres	For minor illnesses or injuries like rashes, earaches, sore throats, or sprains.
NHS 111	Call or use the website when you're unsure where to go. They can direct you or arrange urgent care.
A&E (Accident & Emergency)	For serious or life-threatening conditions like chest pain, breathing problems, or heavy bleeding.
999	For immediate emergencies such as unconsciousness, suspected heart attacks, or severe injuries.

What NHS Services Cost and What They Cover

Here's a general idea of what is free and what may involve charges:

GP appointments	Free
Hospital treatment	Free (if referred or in emergencies)
Prescriptions in England	£9.35 per item (free in Scotland, Wales, and Northern Ireland).
Dental treatment in England	Costs vary by treatment band (£27.80, £78.50, £284.30).
Eye tests	Free for under-16s, over-60s, and those on certain benefits; otherwise, usually £25 to £40.
Healthcare equipment and support aids	This includes items like crutches, hearing aids, or continence products. Some are provided free by the NHS if needed, while others may require a prescription or a small charge.

If you're on a low income or receive certain benefits, you may qualify for help with these costs. Ask your pharmacist or GP surgery about the NHS Low Income Scheme or exemption certificates.

CHAPTER 6

GETTING AROUND: DRIVING, PUBLIC TRANSPORT, AND STAYING LEGAL

Getting around in the UK becomes much easier once you understand how the systems work. Whether you're driving, using public transport, cycling, or walking, knowing the rules helps you stay safe, confident, and within the law. This chapter explains the essentials: how to drive legally, check your insurance, learn to drive, and use public and alternative transport options.

Driving in the UK: What You Need to Know

If you plan to drive in the UK, it's vital to ensure you have a valid driving licence. Some foreign licences are accepted for a limited time depending on the country of issue, but long-term residents usually need to exchange their licence or apply for a UK one through the Driver and Vehicle Licensing Agency (DVLA). Before you drive any vehicle, you must make sure it is insured, taxed, and has passed its MOT if it's over three years old. You also need to ensure the address on your licence and vehicle registration is up-to-date.

Driving a car that is not roadworthy or insured can result in severe penalties, including fines, points on your licence, or even the seizure of your vehicle. It's not just about following rules; it's about protecting yourself and others.

Don't Just Assume You're Insured

One of the most common mistakes drivers make is assuming they are insured when they're not. In the UK, insurance is specific to both the driver and the vehicle. Just because someone permits you to drive their car doesn't mean you're legally allowed to do so. Unless your name is listed on the insurance policy or your own insurance policy explicitly permits you to drive other vehicles, you are not covered. Many policies, particularly cheaper ones or those for new drivers, do not include this kind of cover at all.

It's also important to understand that the "drive other cars" (DOC) feature, when it does exist, often only provides third-party coverage and is usually restricted to occasional situations and not for the regular driving of other cars. Never rely on assumptions. Always check the policy wording, and if in doubt, contact the insurer directly.

You can also check whether a vehicle is insured by using the free tool at askMID.com. This will only tell you whether the car is insured, not whether you are insured to drive it. You must go further to confirm your specific cover.

Having been involved in summary justice in the UK, I've seen first-hand how easy it is for well-meaning people to end up in court simply because they didn't double-check their insurance. They often believed they were doing nothing wrong, driving a family member's car with verbal permission or assuming they were covered under someone else's policy. But under UK law, driving without valid insurance is a criminal offence and is dealt with seriously.

The consequences can be severe. A person caught driving without insurance can receive a £300 fixed penalty and six points on their driving licence. The police can seize and even destroy the car. In many cases, the matter ends up in court, where penalties can be much higher, especially if the person has a poor driving record or has previously committed similar offences. If you accumulate 12 or more points on your licence, whether through insurance offences, speeding, or other offences such as defective tyres, you can be disqualified from driving altogether, often for six months or more. This is known as a 'totting-up' disqualification and can seriously affect your daily life, especially if you rely on driving for work or family responsibilities.

Learning to Drive the Right Way

If you're new to driving in the UK, the process of getting a full licence starts with applying for a provisional licence through the DVLA. You can then begin learning to drive either with a qualified driving instructor or a friend or family member who meets the legal requirements. They must be over 21 and have held a full UK driving licence for at least three years.

To qualify for a full licence, you must pass two tests. The first is the theory test, which covers road rules and hazard awareness. The second is the practical driving test, where you'll demonstrate your driving ability on real roads. Many people choose to take a few professional lessons, even if they are learning with family, to ensure they are well-prepared for the test and feel confident behind the wheel.

Driving in the UK comes with responsibility. Knowing the rules and building your experience gradually will help you become a safe and competent driver.

Public Transport and Getting Around Without a Car

If you don't drive or simply prefer not to, public transport in the UK is a reliable and widely used option. Buses run frequently in most towns and cities, with discounted passes available for children, students, pensioners, and some benefit claimants. Larger cities also have tram networks and train services that connect to surrounding regions.

In London, the Underground (commonly called "the Tube") is a fast and efficient way to travel, and contactless payment cards or Oyster cards can be used to pay fares. In other parts of the country, contactless cards or mobile apps are commonly accepted. Train journeys, including national rail services, can be planned through apps like Trainline or National Rail Enquiries.

It's worth planning ahead when travelling by train or bus, especially during peak times or when strikes and engineering works are taking place. Booking tickets in advance often helps you get cheaper fares, particularly for longer journeys.

E-Scooters: Insurance and Legal Use

E-scooters are becoming more common on streets and pavements, but it's essential to understand the law before using one. Privately owned e-scooters are illegal to ride on public roads, pavements, and cycle paths in most parts of the UK. You are only allowed to use them on private land with the landowner's permission.

Some cities have approved e-scooter rental schemes as part of official government trials. These are the only e-scooters legally allowed on public roads, but even then, the rules are strict. You must be over 18, hold at least a provisional driving licence, and be aware that insurance is a legal requirement. In these trial schemes, the insurance is usually arranged by the rental provider, but it is still a condition of lawful use. If you own a private e-scooter, you cannot simply get insurance and ride it legally on public roads. Currently, the law does not permit it outside of authorised trials.

Misusing an e-scooter, whether by riding on public roads without authorisation, not having a valid licence, or using one without insurance, can lead to a £300 fine and six penalty points on your driving licence. These offences are treated in the same way as using a car illegally. If you're a young person just starting out, getting six points before you've even passed your driving test can seriously damage your driving record. I've seen cases where people were shocked to learn how seriously the courts deal with this, particularly when it comes to using a vehicle without insurance. These endorsements stay on your record for years and can make your insurance costs skyrocket or even make it difficult to get insured at all.

Always check the legal status of any e-scooter you plan to ride. Just because others are doing it doesn't make it legal or safe.

Motorcycling and Mopeds: What You Need to Know

If you're planning to ride a motorcycle or moped in the UK, you must meet specific legal requirements, even for small, low-powered bikes. The first step for most new riders is completing Compulsory Basic Training (CBT). This is a one-day course that teaches essential riding skills and road safety. It's not a test, but you must complete it successfully to ride on the road legally.

Once you've passed CBT, you can ride a moped (up to 50 cc) or a light motorcycle (up to 125 cc) with L-plates, but you cannot carry passengers or ride on motorways. Your CBT certificate is valid for two years, after which you'll need to either retake it or progress to a full motorcycle licence.

To get a full motorcycle licence, you'll need to pass both a theory test and a two-part practical test (Module 1 off-road and Module 2 on-road) and meet the minimum age requirements for the type of bike you want to ride.

Common mistakes new riders make include assuming that buying a small scooter or moped means you can ride it without training or insurance; this is not true. Some also ride without helmets, which is illegal, or forget to display L-plates after CBT. Others wrongly assume their CBT allows them to carry passengers or ride on fast roads, which it does not.

Helmets are a legal requirement for all motorcycle and moped riders and passengers. You must also make sure your vehicle is taxed, insured, and has a valid MOT if it's more than three years old. Failing to meet these conditions could lead to fines, penalty points, or even having your bike seized.

If you're unsure about your status or next steps, it's always a good idea to check official guidance on gov.uk.

Cycling and Walking

Cycling is a popular and environmentally friendly way to get around. Many areas have dedicated cycle lanes and safe routes. You don't need a licence to ride a bicycle, but you are expected to obey traffic signals and road rules just like any other road user. Riding responsibly helps keep you and others safe. Helmets aren't required by law but are strongly recommended. Your bike must have working brakes and front and rear lights if you're riding at night.

Walking is another excellent way to get around, particularly in towns and cities with pedestrian-friendly layouts. Pay attention to crossings, and if you have children, teach them basic road safety, looking both ways, crossing at designated spots, and understanding traffic signals.

Staying Safe and Informed

To stay safe and avoid fines or disqualification, keep up to date with the rules of the road. The Highway Code is available online and in print, and it's worth reviewing regularly even if you've been driving for years. Local councils also publish information about congestion charges, low-emission zones, and parking regulations.

Using apps like Google Maps or Waze can help you plan your journey and avoid road closures or traffic delays. These apps provide real-time traffic updates and route planning features.

If you drive in central London, be aware that you may need to pay the Congestion Charge or meet ULEZ (Ultra Low Emission Zone) standards. Failure to comply could result in automatic fines, with cameras used to monitor and enforce these charges.

CHAPTER 7

EDUCATION AND TRAINING IN THE UK

Education plays a central role in life in the UK, whether you're raising children or building your own skills. The country offers a well-structured school system for children, along with a wide range of lifelong learning opportunities for adults who want to retrain, gain new qualifications, or change careers. This chapter explains how the education system works, how to apply for school places, what support is available for families, and the options available for adult education at every stage of life.

The UK Education System: Key Stages

The education journey in the UK is divided into several stages:

Early Years (ages 0–5)	Nursery and preschool education for young children. Eligible families can access 15 or 30 hours of free childcare per week.
Primary School (ages 4 or 5 to 11)	Full-time education begins here, covering Key Stages 1 and 2.
Secondary School (ages 11 to 16)	Pupils study Key Stages 3 and 4, with GCSE exams at the end of Year 11.
Post-16 Education (ages 16 to 18)	Young people must remain in education or training. Options include A-levels, vocational courses (like BTECs or T Levels), or apprenticeships.

Higher Education (usually 18+)	University degrees and other advanced qualifications, including foundation courses.

Applying for a School Place

Local councils manage school admissions, and applications must be submitted well in advance of the school year.

- **Application Deadlines:**
  - Primary school applications are usually due by mid-January.
  - Secondary school applications typically close by the end of October.
- **Choosing a School:**
  - Parents can express preferences, but places are allocated based on catchment area, availability, and admissions criteria.
- **Relocating Families:**
  - If you're moving into or within the UK, apply early. School places aren't automatic, and waiting lists may apply.

Visit your local council's website to find application forms, deadlines, and school catchment area information.

Support for School-Age Children

There are several forms of support available for children and their families:

Free School Meals	Available to eligible families receiving certain benefits. Apply through your local authority.
Pupil Premium	Additional school funding for disadvantaged pupils. This is allocated to schools automatically but may require proof of eligibility.
Special Educational Needs (SEN)	Children who need extra support may qualify for an Education, Health, and Care Plan (EHCP). Speak to the school's SEN coordinator for guidance.
School Transport	Free or subsidised travel may be provided if the nearest suitable school is beyond a certain distance.

Adult Education and Training

Education doesn't stop after school. Adults over 19 have many opportunities to continue learning:

Adult Community Education	Local councils and colleges offer affordable or free part-time courses in everything from basic literacy to creative arts.
Functional Skills	Qualifications in English, maths, and IT that are practical and widely recognised by employers.

ESOL Courses (English for Speakers of Other Languages)	Low-cost or free English classes to help non-native speakers integrate and improve their communication skills.
Apprenticeships	Open to people aged 16 and over, these combine paid work with study and can lead to professional qualifications.
National Careers Service	Offers free advice on training, job applications, CVs, and more. Visit nationalcareers.service.gov.uk.

Higher Education and University

If you're considering university, the application process typically goes through UCAS (Universities and Colleges Admissions Service).

- **Applying through UCAS:**
  You can apply to up to five courses using one online application. Requirements vary depending on the course and university.
  - Applications open in September.
  - The main deadline is in January for courses starting the following autumn.
  - Visit ucas.com for full guidance.

- **Home vs. Overseas Student Fees:**
  - **Home students** (UK residents for at least 3 years) pay up to £9,250 per year.
  - **Overseas students** may pay between £10,000 and £38,000 depending on the course.

    Unsure of your fee status? Visit ukcisa.org.uk or contact your chosen university.

- **Funding and Student Finance:**
  - **Tuition Fee Loan:** Covers course fees and is paid directly to the university.
  - **Maintenance Loan:** Helps with living costs and is paid into your bank account.

    Repayments begin only when your income goes above a certain threshold (e.g., £25,000/year in 2025) at a rate of 9% on the amount above the threshold.

    Apply at gov.uk/student-finance.

- **Scholarships and Additional Support:**
  Universities and charities offer financial support such as bursaries or grants, based on income, academic performance, or personal circumstances (e.g., care leavers, first in family to attend university).

- **Mature and Part-Time Students:**

Many universities welcome students aged 21+ who may not have traditional qualifications. Options include access to HE diplomas, foundation years, part-time courses, or distance learning with institutions like the Open University.

Paying for Courses and Training

Many adult learning courses are free or heavily subsidised, especially for those who are unemployed or on low incomes. If you're pursuing a higher-level qualification, you may be eligible for an Advanced Learner Loan. For higher education, Student Finance England may help cover tuition and living costs, depending on your situation.

Understanding UK Qualifications

UK education offers a mix of academic and vocational qualifications that suit different paths:

- **Common UK qualifications:**
  GCSEs, A-levels, BTECs, T Levels, NVQs, HNDs, and university degrees.
- **Vocational training** is widely respected and often leads directly to employment.
- **Overseas qualifications:**
  If you have international qualifications, check how they're recognised in the UK through UK ENIC (formerly NARIC).

Avoid Scams

With more learning options available online and in the community, it's vital to stay alert to misleading offers or training scams. Some private companies offer expensive courses that don't lead to recognised qualifications, or they may pressure you into paying before you've had time to check the details.

To protect yourself:

- **Check the provider is genuine** - Use official websites like Ofsted, UCAS, or the National Careers Service to confirm that the course or institution is registered.
- **Avoid large upfront payments** - Be wary of providers asking for big fees in advance without a clear refund policy or written agreement.
- **Verify qualifications** - Not all courses lead to recognised qualifications. Check if the course is accredited by a UK awarding body through Ofqual or UK ENIC.
- **Read reviews and look for contact details** - Trustworthy organisations have clear information, customer service, and a physical address.

If something feels rushed, vague, or too good to be true, take a step back and double-check before sharing your money or information.

If you think a scam has targeted you:

- Report it to Action Fraud at actionfraud.police.uk or by calling 0300 123 2040.
- You can also report unfair trading to Citizens Advice Consumer Service at 0808 223 1133 or citizensadvice.org.uk.

CHAPTER 8

Parenting and Family Life in the UK

Raising a family in a new country comes with both challenges and rewards. Parenting in the UK can be fulfilling, but it may also feel overwhelming, especially when adapting to a new culture, education system, or set of social expectations. Whether you're raising children on your own, with a partner, or as part of a wider family network, this chapter outlines your rights, responsibilities, and where to turn for support.

Birth, Maternity, and Paternity

When a child is born in the UK, there are legal and practical steps to take:

Registering a birth:

- In England, Wales, and Northern Ireland (within 42 days)
- In Scotland (within 21 days)
- Register at your local register office

Birth certificates:

- You'll receive a short certificate free of charge
- You may need to pay for a full certificate, which includes both parents' details

Parental leave entitlements:

- Statutory Maternity Leave is up to 52 weeks
- Statutory Paternity Leave is up to 2 weeks
- Shared Parental Leave is available to some families

Find up-to-date information at www.gov.uk/browse/child-care-parenting.

Healthcare for Children

Children under 16 are entitled to free NHS care, including:

- GP appointments
- Prescriptions
- Dental checkups
- Eye tests
- Routine immunisations

Health visitors provide support for babies and young children up to age 5, including advice on feeding and weaning, child development and sleep, and safety and emotional well-being.

You can ask your GP practice or local children's centre for help connecting to health visiting services.

Early Years and Childcare

The UK provides free childcare support for many families:

- **Free childcare hours** (England):
  - Some 2-year-olds: 15 hours/week (term time)
  - All 3–4-year-olds: 15 or 30 hours/week, depending on eligibility
- **Types of childcare providers**:
  - Nurseries

- Registered childminders
- Pre-schools

Check eligibility and providers at
www.childcarechoices.gov.uk

Schools and Education

Education in the UK is compulsory for children from the age of 5 to 16, covering Reception through to Year 11. However, many young people continue in some form of education or training until age 18. The school year runs from September to July. It includes several holiday breaks: a half-term in October, a Christmas break in December, a half-term in February, a spring break at Easter, and a longer summer holiday between July and early September.

- **Types of schools**:
  - State schools (free, government-funded)
  - Academies (government-funded, with more independence)
  - Faith schools (linked to a religion)
  - Independent/private schools (charge fees)

Parents can apply through their local council for school places.

Support and Legal Protections for Families

Families in the UK benefit from a range of legal protections and support services aimed at ensuring children's welfare and helping parents overcome challenges. Central to this is the Children Act 1989 and 2004, which establishes the right of every child to be safe, heard, and protected. Local councils must offer early help services to families facing difficulties, and when concerns arise about a child's safety, social services may step in. Importantly, their role is usually to support and work with families.

Discipline and the Law

UK law encourages positive, non-violent parenting.

- Physical punishment is illegal in Scotland and Wales.
- In England and Northern Ireland, mild smacking is not automatically a criminal offence, but authorities may investigate anything that causes injury or concern.

It's best to focus on setting clear boundaries, using open communication, and offering emotional support rather than physical discipline.

Support for Parents

Various sources of support are available for parents and carers, although their availability may differ by area. Common options include:

Children's centres	For families with under-5s, offering play sessions, health advice, and parenting support.
Parenting classes	Either free or low-cost, often run by councils or charities.
Family hubs	Currently expanding across many communities to offer joined-up support for families of all ages.
Drop-in sessions	Informal settings where parents can ask for advice or meet others.

Several national organisations also provide trusted advice and guidance:

- Family Lives - support with parenting challenges, from toddler tantrums to teenage issues.
- Gingerbread - advice and community support for single parents.

You can ask your GP, child's school, or local council to help connect you to the right services in your area.

Child Benefit and Financial Help

Most families can receive Child Benefit, a monthly payment per child.

You may also be eligible for:

- Universal Credit
- Free school meals

- Help with school uniforms or transport
- Tax-Free Childcare

Use a benefits calculator to check your eligibility: www.gov.uk/benefits-calculators

Building Family Life and Community

Family life in the UK is diverse and widely accepted. This includes two-parent households, single-parent families, blended families (where children are part of stepfamilies), and multi-generational homes where grandparents, parents, and children may live together.

Staying involved in your child's education and getting to know your local area can help both you and your family feel more settled. It also supports your child's well-being and development. Here are some simple ways to stay engaged:

- Attend parent-teacher meetings and school events, such as assemblies or performances
- Read school newsletters or emails to keep up with news, dates, and school activities
- Join parent groups, such as class WhatsApp chats or the school's Parent-Teacher Association (PTA)
- Make use of local facilities, including libraries, museums, and leisure centres. Many offer free or low-cost activities during weekends and school holidays.

Even small efforts can help you build stronger relationships with your child's school and community while making everyday life feel more connected and enjoyable.

CHAPTER 9

YOUR RIGHTS, FREEDOMS, AND THE LAW

Knowing your legal rights and freedoms helps protect you from unfair treatment. Living in the UK means being covered by a wide range of laws designed to uphold your dignity, freedom, and safety. These protections apply to everyone, regardless of background, nationality, or personal circumstances.

However, many people, especially those who are new to the UK, may not realise how far these rights go. They affect how you're treated at work, by the police, and even what support you can access when things go wrong.

Understanding your rights won't solve every problem, but it gives you the tools to recognise when something isn't right and the confidence to take action.

This chapter outlines key laws that affect everyday life and explains how to get help if your rights are at risk.

Your Basic Rights Under UK Law

The UK doesn't have a single written constitution, but individual rights are protected through a combination of laws. These include:

- The Human Rights Act 1998, which brings the European Convention on Human Rights into UK law. It protects your right to life, liberty, privacy, freedom of expression, a fair trial, and freedom from inhumane treatment.

- The Equality Act 2010 protects you from discrimination based on protected characteristics like race, sex, religion, disability, age, or sexual orientation.
- Data protection laws, such as the UK General Data Protection Regulation (UK GDPR) and the Data Protection Act 2018, give you the right to access your personal data, know how it's used, and request corrections if needed.

These rights are relevant in everyday life: at work, in school, when accessing healthcare or housing, and when dealing with public services.

Protection from Discrimination

Discrimination can show up in obvious or subtle ways. Examples of discrimination include being denied a job, receiving poorer service, or being mistreated due to one's identity. Under the Equality Act 2010, it is unlawful to discriminate against someone because of:

- Race or ethnicity
- Religion or belief
- Sex or sexual orientation
- Disability
- Age
- Gender reassignment
- Pregnancy or maternity
- Marriage or civil partnership

If you experience discrimination, you have the right to raise a complaint and seek legal remedies. This might involve speaking to your employer, school, or housing provider, or contacting organisations such as the Equality Advisory Support Service (EASS) or ACAS for guidance.

Police Powers: What You Should Know

While the police are here to protect the public, they must follow the law and respect your rights. Understanding what they can and cannot do helps reduce fear and confusion during interactions.

Stop and Search

Police can stop and search you if they have "reasonable grounds" to suspect you are carrying illegal items such as drugs, weapons, or stolen goods. You don't have to give your name or address unless you're being reported for an offence. During a stop and search, you have the right to ask:

- Why are you being stopped
- What they are looking for
- Which law gives them the power to search you

Police must also give you a written record of the search or explain how to get one later.

Arrest and Detention

If you're arrested, you have the right to:

- Know why you're being arrested
- Free legal advice at the police station
- Inform someone of your arrest
- Remain silent (though silence may have legal consequences in some cases)

You can usually be held for up to 24 hours before being charged or released, although this can be extended for more serious offences. Most police officers also wear body-worn cameras, which record their interactions. You can request access to this footage if it involves you.

If you feel that police have treated you unfairly, you can make a complaint through the Independent Office for Police Conduct (IOPC).

Everyday Rights in Action

Your legal rights often come into play in everyday situations, such as renting a flat, attending a job interview, dealing with your employer, or being stopped by the police.

For instance, if your landlord enters your home without notice or permission, they may be violating your right to quiet enjoyment of the property. In such cases, you can raise a concern with your local council or seek legal advice. Similarly, rejection of your job application due to your age or religious dress may be considered unlawful discrimination. You can challenge this through the Equality Advisory Support

Service or an employment tribunal, with guidance from Acas or support from a local law centre.

Access to Legal Help

Legal issues can be stressful and expensive, but free or low-cost help is available across the UK. You do not need to face legal problems alone.

Here are some trusted sources of legal support:

- Citizens Advice (citizensadvice.org.uk)
  Free advice on a wide range of issues, including housing, benefits, employment, and consumer rights.
- Law Centres Network (lawcentres.org.uk)
  Offers free legal advice and sometimes representation, especially for people who cannot afford a solicitor.
- Legal Aid (gov.uk/legal-aid)
  Available for serious issues such as housing problems, domestic abuse, or immigration matters if you meet income eligibility.
- Acas (acas.org.uk)
  Offers help with workplace disputes, rights at work, and employment law.
- Equality Advisory Support Service (EASS)
  Provides free advice if you've been discriminated against or your human rights have been violated.

Chapter 10

Easy-to-Miss Laws; Everyday Mistakes That Can Get You in Trouble

Living in the UK entails being a part of a society based on laws, many of which aim to maintain safety, cleanliness, and fairness in communities. However, not all offences are obvious. Every year, people find themselves facing fines or even court appearances for things they didn't realise were illegal.

Often, it's not intentional wrongdoing but simple misunderstandings that lead to serious consequences. By becoming aware of these lesser-known rules, especially those that can affect newcomers or visitors, you can protect yourself and confidently handle everyday life within the law.

This chapter explains everyday legal mistakes that many people make without realising, from watching live TV without a licence to parking on zigzag lines or leaving a vehicle idling outside a school. Since ignorance is not an excuse under the law, staying informed is key to avoiding unnecessary trouble.

TV Licensing Offences

One of the most common misunderstandings is around TV licensing. Many people assume that if they're watching TV on their laptop or streaming content online, they don't need a licence. However, if you watch or record live television on any channel or use BBC iPlayer, the law says you must have a valid TV licence regardless of how you watch it. In shared accommodation, each flat or unit may need its own licence. For example, someone living in a house with multiple tenants thought their flatmate's licence covered them all, only to receive a fine of over £100 later when a TV licence inspector visited.

Visit www.tvlicensing.co.uk to check if you need a licence.

Fly-Tipping and Illegal Waste Disposal

Leaving rubbish beside bins, in alleyways, or on pavements is classified as fly-tipping. Councils take this seriously and use CCTV or waste inspections to trace items back to the person responsible.

One person left a broken chair by a communal bin after moving house, thinking it would be collected, but later received a penalty notice for fly-tipping. In another case, a person dumped shed rubbish near a public bin and was fined £400 after inspectors found their name on packaging inside a bag.

Importantly, if you pay someone to remove your rubbish and they dump it illegally, you could still be held responsible. The law requires you to check that anyone you hire is a registered waste carrier; you can be fined if they fly-tip your waste.

Always use proper disposal methods or licensed services. Fly-tipping is a criminal offence that may lead to heavy fines or prosecution.

Book a bulky waste collection through your local council or take items to a licensed recycling centre.

Littering, Including Throwing Items from Cars

Littering may seem like a minor issue, but even small acts can attract a fixed penalty notice or prosecution. Disposing of items like cigarette butts, chewing gum, or food packaging in public places is a criminal offence in many areas of the UK. This includes throwing rubbish from a car window or leaving waste beside an already full public bin. Councils actively monitor this behaviour through street patrols and mobile CCTV, and they have the authority to issue fines on the spot. Penalties typically range from £80 to £150. In one case, someone tossed a sandwich wrapper from a car window, unaware that a CCTV van was nearby. A few days later, the vehicle's registered keeper received a £150 fixed penalty notice through the post.

Dispose of litter in public bins or take it home. Be especially cautious near high streets, parks, or roads.

Parking on Pavements or Zigzag Lines

In many parts of the UK, especially London, parking rules are stricter than people usually realise. For example, parking on the pavement is generally prohibited unless clearly permitted by signage. Stopping or parking on white or yellow zigzag lines near pedestrian crossings or schools is also a serious offence, even if it's just for a minute. These markings are there to protect pedestrians by keeping sight lines clear. One person who briefly stopped on zigzag lines outside a school returned to find a parking ticket on their windscreen, despite only being away for "two minutes." Even short stops can lead to fines, so it's essential to know the rules wherever you park.

Always check the road markings and nearby signs before parking. Don't assume a quick stop is allowed.

Playing Loud Music at Night

Everyone has the right to enjoy peace and quiet in their home. Excessive noise late at night, whether from music, parties, shouting, or barking dogs, can be classed as a statutory nuisance under the Environmental Protection Act. One tenant assumed it was acceptable to play music until midnight, but after receiving ongoing complaints from neighbours, the local council intervened. Monitoring equipment was installed, and when the disturbances continued, a noise abatement notice was issued. Breaching the notice resulted in a £200 fine.

Keep noise low after 11 p.m. and respond calmly to any neighbours' complaints. Councils can investigate and act.

Driving Someone Else's Car

It's easy to assume that if a car has insurance, you're covered to drive it, but that's not always the case. Insurance is typically linked to the individual, not just the vehicle. If you're borrowing someone else's car, you need to ensure you're either named on their insurance policy or have your own coverage that allows you to drive other vehicles. Many policies don't cover this, so it's crucial to check before getting behind the wheel.

For instance, a person borrowed a family member's car for a quick errand and was stopped by the police. The police discovered the driver wasn't listed on the car's insurance policy. As a result, the driver was fined, received six penalty points, and had the car seized. The lesson here is that it's not enough to rely on the car being insured. Your own insurance coverage matters too.

Commuting and Insurance Coverage

Another common mistake is assuming that a "Social, Domestic and Pleasure" insurance policy covers commuting to work. This type of policy typically only covers personal, non-work-related driving. If your job involves driving to and from a fixed workplace, you'll need to ensure your insurance policy specifically includes commuting. Without this coverage, you could face penalties for driving illegally.

Make sure to check your policy and, if necessary, update it to include commuting. This simple step can help avoid unnecessary legal trouble down the road.

Not Updating Vehicle or Address Details

Failing to update your driving licence or vehicle logbook (V5C) with the DVLA is more than just an admin oversight; it's a legal requirement. If you move to a new house without notifying the DVLA about your new address, you could potentially miss important notifications such as penalty notices, speeding fines, or even court summons. This can lead to fines of up to £1,000.

One individual experienced this first-hand when they relocated to a new residence and neglected to update their vehicle registration. A speeding notice sent to their old address went unanswered, which led to a court hearing they weren't even aware of and a hefty fine issued in their absence.

Keeping your address up to date with the DVLA and other key services, like your local council, is a small task that can save you from major legal trouble.

Visit www.gov.uk/dvla to update your address or vehicle details.

Using E-scooters on Public Roads

Privately owned e-scooters are currently not legal for use on public roads, pavements, or cycle lanes in the UK. The only exception is if you're using one through a government-approved rental trial, and even then, riders must follow road rules and have the correct insurance.

Many people are unaware that e-scooters remain restricted in most areas. In London, Transport for London (TfL) has also banned them from trains and buses due to safety concerns, particularly the risk of battery fires.

Don't assume e-scooters are treated like bicycles. Always check local laws before riding one in public.

Carrying Offensive Weapons Without Realising

Some items, like certain knives, pepper spray, or heavy tools, can be considered offensive weapons under UK law if carried in public without a valid reason. This is especially important in sensitive locations like schools, train stations, or airports, where the rules are even stricter.

Someone once kept a multi-tool in their backpack, unaware that the locking blade it contained was illegal to possess in public. Police stopped them during a routine bag check at a train station and issued a caution for carrying a bladed article.

Avoid carrying any sharp objects unless you have a legitimate reason. Check UK knife laws at www.gov.uk.

Dog Fouling and Control Orders

Local councils take dog fouling seriously and enforce regulations through fines and surveillance. Failing to clean up after your dog in public spaces, including parks, pavements, and grass verges, can lead to a fixed penalty notice. In many areas, Public Space Protection Orders (PSPOs) also require dogs to be kept on leads in designated zones.

A dog owner, who regularly walked their pet late at night, believed they wouldn't attract attention if they left the mess behind. Weeks later, a fixed penalty notice arrived; CCTV near the local park had clearly captured the incident.

Today, many public spaces are monitored by cameras, and fines can be issued based on footage or community reports, even if no one approaches you at the time. Enforcement continues around the clock.

Always carry dog waste bags and check for PSPO signage when entering parks or other public areas to ensure compliance with the law. Clean up after your dog; it's your responsibility and ignoring it can have real consequences.

CHAPTER 11

Settling into Your Local Area and Enjoying Everyday Life

Moving to a new area can be exciting, but it can also take time to feel truly at home. This chapter will help you enjoy your local area, whether you're working, studying, or raising a family. From finding community spaces to understanding local services, it's about settling in, feeling connected, and building a life that works for you.

Getting to Know Your Area

Start by exploring your neighbourhood on foot or using public transportation. Notice where the key places are: your GP's surgery, the local pharmacy, the post office, the town centre, and nearby green spaces. Libraries, parks, leisure centres, markets, and community hubs are often central to local life.

Many areas have a local newsletter, Facebook group, or WhatsApp community noticeboard where people share updates, events, recommendations, and alerts. It's a wonderful way to get a feel for the area and discover what's happening nearby.

Local Amenities That Can Make Life Easier

Once you're settled, it's worth knowing what's available close to home. Here are a few amenities to look out for:

- **Libraries** - They're not just for books! Many offer free internet, events for children and adults, homework help, and quiet study areas.

- **Leisure centres** - Local gyms and pools are often subsidised, especially if you live in the area or qualify for a discount.
- **Community centres** - These host classes, meetings, cultural events, support groups, and more.
- **Parks and open spaces** - The UK has many well-kept parks. Look out for community gardens, tennis courts, outdoor gyms, or local walking routes.
- **Markets and local businesses** - Farmers' markets and high streets are good places to meet people, support local traders, and try new foods or crafts.

Exploring these amenities can help you feel more settled and introduce you to different aspects of local culture.

Getting Involved Locally

Joining in with local life is one of the best ways to feel at home. Whether it's volunteering, attending events, or chatting with neighbours, here are some easy ways to get involved:

- Say hello to people at your local shop, library, or on the school run
- Attend local festivals, cultural days, or council-hosted fun days
- Join a walking group, choir, sports club, or community project

- Check your council website for free or low-cost local events
- Offer to help out at your child's school or community centre

You don't need to commit long-term; even occasional involvement can help you build confidence and connections.

Finding Support When You Need It

Life isn't always smooth, especially when you're adjusting to new surroundings. It's good to know where to turn if you need help or advice:

- Local councils offer services like housing advice, recycling, family support, and well-being schemes.
- Citizens Advice can help with benefits, consumer issues, or housing
- Faith groups and places of worship often offer social activities, help for newcomers, and pastoral care
- Community organisations may run food banks, budgeting support, mental health groups, or English conversation classes

You're not alone; there are usually people and places ready to help if you ask.

Enjoying Local Life Through the Seasons

The UK has a rich calendar of local and national traditions. From fireworks in November to summer carnivals, Easter fairs, Diwali lights, and Christmas markets, there's often something happening in your area.

Get familiar with seasonal routines too:

- In spring and summer, many towns hold fairs, outdoor theatre, or sports days
- In autumn, you'll find harvest festivals and local exhibitions
- Winter often includes Christmas light switch-ons, festive events, and indoor markets

Celebrating local customs and public holidays is a delightful way to feel part of the wider community.

Tips to Feel More at Home

- Explore different walking routes or cycle paths. Notice the local architecture, greenery, and public art.
- Visit nearby towns or villages for a change of scenery,
- Get to know your neighbours. A smile and a short conversation can go a long way.
- Learn about the history of your area. Local museums or plaques often tell fascinating stories.
- Try local cafes, bakeries, or other local eateries. You may discover your new favourite treat.

Key Contacts to Save

Make sure you know who to call if something happens. These are the main services to be aware of:

Service	Phone Number	When to Use
Emergency services (Police, Fire, Ambulance)	999	Life-threatening emergencies
Non-emergency police	101	Reporting crime or concerns that are not urgent
NHS 24/7 helpline	111	When you need medical advice but it's not an emergency
Gas emergency service	0800 111 999	If you smell gas or suspect a carbon monoxide leak
Local council	Varies by area	Report housing, street safety, noise, rubbish, and more

Add these numbers to your phone and write them down in a visible location at home.

CHAPTER 12

British Life and Everyday Culture

Understanding local customs and social norms can help you feel more comfortable and included. Settling into a new place isn't just about finding your way around; it's also about picking up on the everyday habits and values that shape how people live and interact. Much of British culture is unspoken, rooted in subtle social cues and routines. If you weren't raised here, it may feel unfamiliar at first, but with time and observation, it becomes second nature.

One of the first things people notice is the emphasis on politeness. Saying "please" and "thank you" is expected in almost every interaction, whether at the supermarket, on the bus, or when asking for directions. Apologising when you bump into someone, even if it wasn't your fault, is a common courtesy. Holding doors open, letting others off public transport before boarding, and waiting your turn in a queue are all small but meaningful ways to show respect. While not everyone follows these perfectly, ignoring them can seem rude, even if that's not your intention.

This chapter outlines the unwritten rules and everyday behaviours that are common in the UK. You'll learn about social expectations, manners, and cultural norms that can help you feel more confident at work, school, in your neighbourhood, or during daily activities.

Everyday Manners and Politeness

- Say “please” and “thank you” regularly, even with strangers is a basic but important part of British politeness.
- Apologise for minor accidents, like bumping into someone, for example.
- Queuing is an essential part of British culture; always wait your turn in line.
- Hold doors open for others, especially in public places is appreciated.
- Let people get off public transport before getting on.
- Turning your back on someone can be seen as rude. Body language should show attentiveness, especially when someone is speaking to you.
- Addressing people politely, using titles like "Mr.", "Mrs.", or "Miss" when you first meet them, shows respect.

Greeting people is generally informal. A simple “hi,” “hello,” or “morning” is typical, and while handshakes may still appear in professional settings, they’re not expected day to day. Personal space is valued, especially in queues or on public transport, and standing too close might make others feel uncomfortable. Making eye contact when speaking shows confidence and politeness, but staring is usually avoided.

Building Connections and Respecting Personal Space

In the UK, people often appear reserved at first, but this doesn't mean they're unfriendly. Friendships tend to grow gradually through consistent, everyday interactions, like chatting at the school gate, sharing a laugh at work, or greeting neighbours regularly.

Personal space and social cues matter

- Greet people casually with "Hi," "Hello," or "Morning," especially in local shops or familiar settings.
- Maintain natural eye contact but avoid staring.
- Give others space in queues and on public transport; standing too close can feel uncomfortable.

When building friendships or socialising

- An invitation to coffee, the pub, or someone's home is a sincere expression of trust.
- Arrive on time or message if you're running late. Punctuality shows respect.
- Bring a small gift when visiting someone's home. Flowers, snacks, or a soft drink are thoughtful gestures.
- Friendships develop slowly. Be consistent, kind, and open. Familiarity builds over time.

Public Behaviour and Shared Spaces

Courtesy and respect for others are central to life in shared environments. Whether you're living in a flat, using public transport, or walking through your neighbourhood, some common expectations help everyone get along:

- Keep noise to a minimum, particularly at night or in buildings with thin walls.
- Always dispose of rubbish properly. Littering is taken seriously and may result in fines.
- Use calm and respectful language in public. Shouting or using offensive words may be considered threatening or antisocial.
- Follow public rules such as queuing and waiting at pedestrian crossings. Give others personal space, especially in busy areas.

These simple behaviours help maintain a safe and considerate environment for all.

Dress and Everyday Appearance

In the UK, there is no national dress code, and individuals typically wear what they find comfortable; however, the context of the situation can influence their choices.

- Work settings may require smart casual or formal dress, depending on the job.

- Schools usually have uniforms for children from primary to secondary level.
- Religious buildings or formal events may expect modest or respectful clothing.

You'll notice a wide variety of personal styles, especially in larger cities, so individuality is generally welcomed.

Religion, Belief, and Inclusivity

The UK is multicultural and protects freedom of religion and belief through law. People are generally expected to be respectful of others' beliefs, even if they don't share them.

- Halal, kosher, vegan, and vegetarian options are widely available in supermarkets and restaurants.
- Schools, workplaces, and local events often acknowledge major religious festivals like Eid, Diwali, Hanukkah, and Christmas.
- Many employers and schools will try to accommodate prayer times, fasting, or faith-related requests, particularly if informed in advance.

Cultural Values to Keep in Mind

Certain values shape daily life in the UK and help explain how people interact:

- **Fairness:** People expect equal treatment. Jumping a queue or asking for special favours is likely to cause upsets.
- **Privacy:** People tend to keep personal matters to themselves. Avoid asking about topics like money, immigration status, or relationships unless you know someone well.
- **Humour:** British humour often uses understatement, irony, or sarcasm. If someone says, "Not bad," they may actually mean "very good."
- **Modesty:** It's common for people to downplay their achievements or make fun of themselves rather than show off.

Understanding these values can help you interpret social cues and build trust more easily.

CHAPTER 13

Faith, Belief, and Inclusion in the UK

The UK is a diverse and multicultural society where people from many different religious and non-religious backgrounds live side by side. Freedom of religion and belief is protected by law, and most people are free to practice their faith openly or to live without religious belief.

This chapter explores how religion and belief are recognised in public life, how different faiths and worldviews are accommodated in schools, workplaces, and communities, and what legal protections exist to ensure everyone is treated fairly and respectfully, regardless of their background. It also highlights how inclusion and understanding play a role in building a cohesive society where all beliefs are valued.

Freedom of Religion and Belief

Your right to follow a religion, or not, is protected under the Human Rights Act 1998 and the Equality Act 2010. This includes:

- Practising or choosing not to practise a religion
- Wearing religious dress or symbols (subject to safety and workplace policies)
- Attending places of worship or religious gatherings
- Changing or leaving your religion without penalty

Discrimination based on religion or belief is unlawful in areas like work, education, housing, and public services.

Faith in Daily Life

People in the UK live out their beliefs in many ways. You'll find churches, mosques, synagogues, temples, gurdwaras, and other places of worship across the country. Many communities also celebrate faith-based festivals such as:

- Christmas (Christian)
- Eid al-Fitr and Eid al-Adha (Muslim)
- Diwali (Hindu, Sikh, Jain)
- Hanukkah (Jewish)
- Vesak (Buddhist)

These festivals are often marked publicly and may include school or local events that reflect the diversity of the community.

Religion and Education

In state-funded schools in England and Wales, Religious Education (RE) is part of the curriculum. This teaching usually covers a range of world religions and ethical worldviews. Daily collective worship is required by law; however, parents have the option to withdraw their children if they wish.

Some schools are faith-based, such as Church of England, Catholic, or Islamic schools, and may prioritise admission for children of that faith. However, these schools must still teach the national curriculum and operate within national guidelines.

Scotland and Northern Ireland have different arrangements, but religion remains part of their education systems. Ask your child's school for clarification if you have any questions about the lessons they are receiving.

Belief in the Workplace

Employers are legally required to treat employees fairly, regardless of their religion or belief. Reasonable workplace adjustments may include:

- Flexible breaks for religious observance
- Permission to wear religious clothing or symbols
- Access to a quiet space for prayer or reflection

These adjustments should be balanced with business needs and health and safety requirements. If you feel you have been treated unfairly, speak to your HR department or trade union, or contact ACAS (Advisory, Conciliation and Arbitration Service) for free advice.

More information: www.acas.org.uk/religion-or-belief-discrimination

Interfaith and Community Inclusion

Across the UK, interfaith organisations promote dialogue, cooperation, and understanding among people of different faiths and beliefs. These initiatives help reduce prejudice and build stronger communities.

You may wish to get involved in:

- Local interfaith events
- Cultural festivals or community meals
- Open days at mosques, temples, churches, or gurdwaras
- School or youth discussions about belief and inclusion

These events are open to people of all backgrounds and are a wonderful way to learn, share, and connect.

Faith and Public Services

Public institutions in the UK usually take steps to meet religious and spiritual needs. For example:

- Hospitals and universities often have multi-faith chaplains or prayer spaces
- Prisons, the armed forces, and care homes provide for religious observance and pastoral care
- Public services may be able to meet dietary needs (such as halal, kosher, or vegetarian meals) when requested

Hate Crime and Reporting

Religious or belief-based hate crime is taken seriously in the UK. This includes:

- Verbal abuse or threats

- Harassment or bullying
- Damage to religious property or places of worship
- Online abuse

You can report a hate crime by:

- Calling 999 in an emergency
- Calling 101 for non-emergency support
- Using the True Vision website: www.report-it.org.uk

Many charities and faith-based organisations provide help and support for those affected.

CHAPTER 14

LIVING WELL AND CONTRIBUTING TO SOCIETY IN THE UK

Living well means more than just getting by; it's about building a life where you can truly thrive. Life in the UK is not only about following the rules or accessing services. It also involves understanding how to participate in society, connect with others, and shape a meaningful life rooted in shared values. Whether you are here for work, study, family, or refuge, you are part of a wider community, and your presence, efforts, and voice all matter.

This final chapter invites you to take an active role in your community and to think about how you can contribute in ways that enrich both your own life and the lives of those around you. It offers practical suggestions for living well and getting involved, especially if you plan to settle in the UK long-term. It also reflects the UK government's integration goals, which highlight the importance of inclusion, civic participation, mutual respect, and shared responsibility.

Understanding Integration

The UK's approach to integration encourages migrants to become active participants in their communities, not only by meeting legal requirements (like language, residency, and financial stability), but also by building relationships, taking part in local life, and contributing positively to society.

While contributing to your community is not a legal requirement for most visas, it is strongly encouraged in the broader integration policy and can be part of what is considered good character, especially for those applying for Indefinite Leave to Remain or British citizenship.

What Does It Mean to Contribute to Society?

You don't need to be wealthy, highly educated, or in a public position to contribute meaningfully to UK society. Contribution can take many forms and often starts with everyday actions:

- Being a respectful and helpful neighbour
- Supporting your child's school, places of worship, or charities
- Taking part in local events, consultations, or community meetings
- Voting in elections if you are eligible
- Joining local efforts to improve your area, such as food banks or youth groups

These actions help build social trust and create a sense of belonging, both for you and for others. They also align with the UK's values of democracy, fairness, and mutual respect.

Volunteering and Community Involvement

Volunteering is one of the most recognised ways to contribute to your community. It also helps you meet people, improve your language skills, build experience, and feel more connected to local life. Volunteering can also be useful if you're new to the UK job market, helping to build local experience and references.

You can volunteer with:

- Local charities
- Youth groups and sports clubs
- Hospitals and care homes
- Libraries, parks, and community centres
- Online causes and helplines

You can also find opportunities on websites like **www.ncvo.org.uk** or **www.volunteeringmatters.org.uk**, or through your local council's website.

Looking After Yourself and Those Around You

Living well starts with looking after yourself and looking out for others when you can. Support is readily available in the UK, and people view taking care of their health and well-being as a strength rather than a burden.

Here's how you can stay well and connected:

- Look after your health: Regular check-ups, getting enough rest, eating well, and staying active all make a difference. If something doesn't feel right, don't wait; the NHS is here for you.

- Reach out when you need to: Whether it's physical or mental health, help is available. Your GP is a great first step, or you can call NHS 111 for guidance.
- Support those around you: If you're caring for a child, elderly relative, or someone with extra needs, your role matters. You're not alone. Many people are informal carers, and there's support available. Visit www.carersuk.org to explore advice, benefits, and community resources.

And if life feels overwhelming:

- Mind - Find practical mental health support: www.mind.org.uk
- Samaritans - Someone to talk to, 24/7: Call 116 123 (free)

Looking after yourself helps you live fully and makes it easier to care for others, too. It's a vital part of living well in the UK.

Taking Part in Public Life

You don't need a political background to get involved in civic life. In the UK, public roles are open to people from all walks of life, and everyday citizens play a vital role in shaping their communities.

Being active means using your voice, time, or experience to help improve local services, represent community interests, or support decision-making processes. This isn't just for politicians; it's for parents, workers, students, retirees, and anyone who cares about where they live.

Ways to get involved include:

- Voting in local and national elections (if eligible). British citizens, Irish citizens, and some Commonwealth residents can vote in most elections.
- Contacting your local councillor or attending council meetings to raise issues that matter to you.
- Consider joining a school governing body or parent-teacher association to help shape local education.
- Participating in consultations or signing petitions on local or national matters.
- Standing for a public role, such as becoming a councillor, trustee, or board member of a voluntary organisation.

To check your voting eligibility and register, visit www.gov.uk/register-to-vote.

Getting involved helps ensure decisions reflect the needs of the whole community, not just the loudest voices. It's a powerful way to belong, contribute, and make change happen.

Supporting Others and Strengthening Community

Contributing to society also means helping to create a welcoming and inclusive environment for those around you. In a diverse country like the UK, mutual respect and everyday cooperation are essential for strong, connected communities.

You can make a meaningful difference by:

- Welcoming new neighbours or residents, especially those who are new to the area or country
- Taking part in local events that bring people together, such as community fairs, interfaith gatherings, or cultural celebrations
- Supporting causes that promote fairness, anti-racism, equality, or access to opportunities for all
- Helping to bridge differences, for example, translating for someone, explaining how a local service works, or simply listening to others' experiences
- Speaking up calmly and respectfully when you notice exclusion, unfairness, or misinformation

Even small actions, such as introducing yourself, offering help, or learning about someone's background, can help build trust and shared goals.

Glossary

ACAS
Advisory, Conciliation and Arbitration Service. The service offers free advice on workplace rights and assists in resolving disputes between employers and employees.

Asylum Seeker
A person who has applied for protection as a refugee but whose claim has not yet been decided.

Benefits
Government financial support for unemployed people, those on low income, those who are disabled, or those facing specific circumstances (e.g., housing needs, childcare).

Biometric Residence Permit (BRP)
A card that proves your immigration status and right to work, study, or access services in the UK.

British Values
Principles such as democracy, rule of law, individual liberty, mutual respect, and tolerance of different beliefs.

Carer
A person who looks after someone with a physical or mental health need. They may be a family member, friend, or professional.

Citizens Advice
A UK charity offering free advice on legal, financial, housing, immigration, and consumer issues.

Council Tax
A local charge collected by councils to fund services like waste collection, libraries, and social care.

Credit Score
A number based on your financial history that shows how likely you are to repay debt. It is often checked when renting or applying for a loan.

Discrimination
Unfair treatment of a person or group based on characteristics such as race, age, gender, disability, religion, or sexual orientation. In many cases, this is against the law under the Equality Act 2010, especially in areas like employment, education, housing, and public services.

Driving Licence
A legal document that proves your right to drive in the UK. You must meet requirements, pass tests, and follow specific rules.

DVLA
Driver and Vehicle Licensing Agency. Responsible for driver licences and vehicle registrations in Great Britain.

Employment Contract
A legal agreement outlining your job terms, including pay, working hours, and duties.

Equality Act 2010
A law protecting people from discrimination based on age, disability, gender, race, religion, sexual orientation, and more.

GP (General Practitioner)
This is your local doctor. Registering with a GP allows you to access NHS healthcare, referrals, and prescriptions.

Gross Pay
Your total earnings before tax and other deductions.

HMRC
His Majesty's Revenue and Customs is the department that handles taxes, National Insurance, and some benefits.

Housing Association
Non-profit organisations providing affordable rental homes. Tenancy terms may differ from those of private landlords.

Integration
Becoming part of a community or society, often by learning the language, accessing services, working, and participating locally.

Legal Aid
Free or low-cost legal advice and representation for people who meet certain financial or case-specific criteria.

Local Authority
Your local council, responsible for services like housing, social care, roads, and education.

Minimum Wage / Living Wage
The legal minimum pay per hour set by the government. The living wage (not mandatory) is a higher rate promoted as more realistic for covering basic costs.

MOT (Ministry of Transport Test)
An annual vehicle safety test required for most cars over 3 years old in the UK.

National Insurance (NI)
A system of contributions paid by workers and employers to fund state benefits such as pensions and maternity leave.

NI Number (National Insurance Number)
Your unique personal number is used to track work and contributions. It is needed for work, taxes, and some benefits.

NHS
National Health Service. The publicly funded healthcare system in the UK, mostly free at the point of use.

Pay As You Earn (PAYE)
The system where employers deduct income tax and National Insurance from your wages before you're paid.

Private Renting
Renting a property from an individual or company landlord (not the council or a housing association).

Public Transport
Buses, trains, trams, and other services open to the public and usually run by local authorities or private operators.

Refugee
A person granted legal protection in the UK because it is unsafe to return to their home country.

Right to Work
The legal status that allows someone to be employed in the UK. Employers are required to check this before hiring.

Safeguarding
Protecting children and vulnerable adults from abuse, neglect, or exploitation.

Self-Employed
You work for yourself, often as a freelancer, sole trader, or contractor. You are responsible for submitting your own taxes and do not get paid through PAYE.

Settlement / Settled Status
Immigration status that gives you the right to stay in the UK permanently (after a certain period of residence).

Starting a Business
Setting up a company or enterprise. This may involve registering with Companies House, opening a business bank account, and hiring others. It's different from being self-employed in scale and legal structure.

Statutory
Something required by law, e.g., statutory maternity pay, statutory sick pay.

Tenancy Agreement
A legal contract between landlord and tenant stating the terms and responsibilities of renting a home.

Universal Credit
A monthly benefit payment to help with living costs, replacing several older benefits. Paid to people who are working on a low income or are out of work.

Volunteering
Giving your time to help others or support a cause, without payment.

Work Permit / Visa
Official permission to work in the UK. Some people may need a visa depending on their immigration status.

Author's Note

This book was written to address a clear gap. Across the UK, people are expected to follow rules, meet requirements, and access services, but the information they need is often scattered, unclear, or hard to find. When you don't know the rules, the consequences can be significant.

Whether it's understanding how renting works, what your rights are at work, how to access healthcare, or how to resolve money issues, people are too often left to figure things out on their own. I've seen this affect newcomers, young adults, long-time residents, and families alike.

Know the Rules UK is my response. It's not a legal manual or a government leaflet. It's a practical guide for real life written in plain language, grounded in everyday experience, and designed to help you feel more confident, informed, and in control.

Use this book as a starting point. Keep it nearby when you need direction, clarity, or reassurance. You don't have to know everything all at once. But you do deserve the tools to live well, avoid costly mistakes, and make the most of life in the UK.

Thank you for reading and for taking the time to understand how things work. Many people may not realise the importance of this step, but it truly makes a significant difference.

If you're ever unsure where to turn, remember that this guide includes links to trusted sources and services throughout each chapter. You can always revisit a section or look up official websites like **www.gov.uk** or Citizens Advice to find practical, up-to-date information. Sometimes the answers are out there, just not always easy to find. I hope this book has made things a little clearer.

Warm wishes,

Bukky Okunade

ALSO BY THE AUTHOR

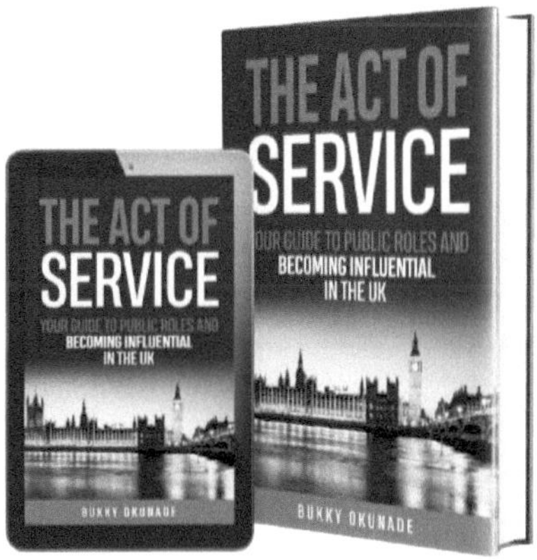

The Act of Service: Your Guide to Public Roles and Becoming Influential in the UK

By Bukky Okunade

This inspiring and practical book shows how everyday people take on public roles and build influence in the UK, whether as school governors, charity trustees, community leaders, or even political candidates.

With clear steps and real-life insight, *The Act of Service* helps you discover your voice, understand how power works, and act with purpose. It's your guide to making a difference at the local or national level, no matter your background.

Available at www.bukkyofficial.com, Amazon, and other bookshops.

www.ingramcontent.com/pod-product-compliance
Ingram Content Group UK Ltd.
Pitfield, Milton Keynes, MK11 3LW, UK
UKHW040225290926
15471UKWH00001B/3

9 781068 465505